The Great Race

Written by Lisa Thompson
Pictures by Craig Smith and Lew Keilar

Captain Red Beard was excited. The Great Pirate Race was to be held the next day.

The crew had been training for weeks. *The Black Beast* was sure to win.

All the ships in the race had to sail out of Pirate Cove, around Skull Rock and back to port.

A dozen ships had entered the race and the competition was fierce.

The first one back to port would be the winner. The prize was a treasure chest full of gold.

Every pirate was determined that his ship would win.

Captain Red Beard and his crew were ready. The cannon boomed and the race was on.

A gust of wind filled *The Black Beast's* sails, and it raced into the lead.

"We're on course to win. Get ready to collect our treasure," said the Captain.

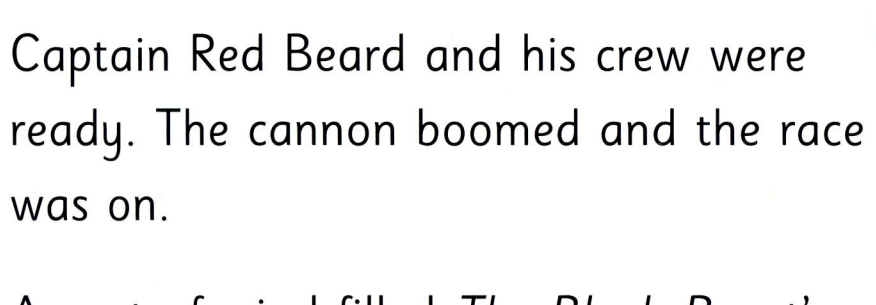

The Black Beast sailed nearer and nearer to Skull Rock. It was a dangerous spot. Many ships were wrecked on its reefs. The crew could see the broken ships in the water. Suddenly there was a giant BOOM near the ship.

"Shiver me timbers!" cried Captain Red Beard. "That was a cannonball."

"It's Nasty Norman on *The Red Dagger*," said Lizzie. "His crew is trying to sink us!"

"Pesky Pirates!" squawked Fingers. "That's cheating! Perfectly Pesky Pirates!"

"They'll have to catch us first," cried Captain Red Beard.

Captain Red Beard steered *The Black Beast* towards Skull Rock.

"Captain, be careful!" cried Lizzie. "We'll be shipwrecked on the rocks!"

Nasty Norman and his crew followed *The Black Beast*.

Boom! Boom! Boom!

Cannonballs flew from *The Red Dagger* and clouds of smoke filled the air.

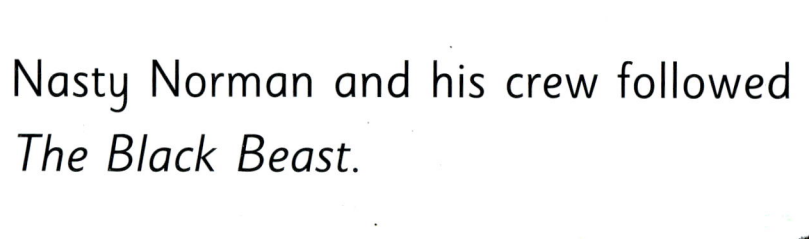

Captain Red Beard smiled a grim smile.

The crew gasped as *The Black Beast* drew closer and closer to Skull Rock. At the last moment, the Captain swung the wheel sharply and *The Black Beast* sailed away to safety.

Nasty Norman and his crew couldn't see where they were going. There was too much smoke around their ship.

They crashed right into Skull Rock.

The Black Beast sailed into Pirate Cove in first place. Captain Red Beard collected the winner's treasure.

But the real reward was watching Nasty Norman and his crew swim back to shore.